An Interactive, Multilingual Counting E

THREE LANGUAGES | TRES IDIOMAS | TROIS LANGUES

3 ENGLISH   ESPAÑOL   FRANÇAIS

REVISED EDITION

JUST GENIOS KIDS
EST. 2020

Animal 123s 1 to 20

Designed by Derville Lowe
Illustrated by Tasha Lowe

NCH
PUBLISHING

This book is designed for children; however, parent participation is highly recommended for optimal usage and learning. Since cognitive development, including numeracy, varies from child to child, the author makes no explicit guarantees or assertions pertaining to the use of this book.

Due to the dynamic nature of the Internet, emails or web addresses used in this book may have changed or been updated after publication and may no longer be valid.

Any photographs, illustrations, imagery or depiction of people used herein are for illustrative purposes only and are not of real people, unless otherwise noted.

Illustrated by Tasha Lowe
Layout, Cover & Interior Design by
NCH Publishing

Books by this author are available on Amazon, through booksellers or by contacting:

Derville Lowe
Vancouver, British Columbia, Canada
derville.lowe@gmail.com
(250) 899-2961

....

Awesome, Let's go! / ¡Estupendo, Vamos! /
Génial, Allons-y!

1

One [won]

Uno [uu-no]

Un [ah]

One little Pig / **Un Cerdito** / **Un Petit Cochon**
[won lit-tle pig]   [un sel-dee-toh]   [ah peh-tee ku-sho]

2

Two [too]
Dos [dos]
Deux [du]

Two Hippos / Dos Hipopótamos / Deux Hippopotames
[too hip-pos]   [dos he-po-po-ta-mos]   [duz he-po-po-tam]

3

Three [th-ree]
Tres [tles]
Trois [twah]

Three Koalas / Tres Koalas / Trois Koalas
[th-ree ko-a-las] [tles ko-a-las] [twah ko-a-la]

4

Four [for]

Cuatro [kua-tlo]

Quatre [kat]

Four Gorillas / Cuatro Gorilas / Quatre Gorilles
[for goh-ri-las]　　　[kua-tlo goh-ree-las]　　　[kat gu-ree]

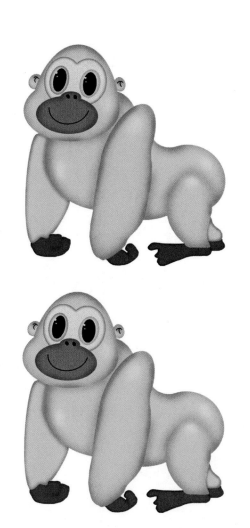

5

Five [fa-iv]
Cinco [sing-ko]
Cinq [sank]

Five Bees / Cinco Abejas / Cinq Abeilles
[fa-iv beez] [sing-ko ah-bae-has] [sank ah-baey]

Six [siks]

Seis [sey-is]

Six [sis]

Six Turtles / Seis Torgugas / Six Tortues
[siks ter-tles] [sey-is tol-too-gas] [sis tok-tyu]

7

Seven [seh-ven]
Siete [see-eh-teh]
Sept [set]

Seven Orcas / Siete Orcas / Sept Orques

[seh-ven or-kas] [see-eh-teh or-kas] [set orks]

8

Eight [ayt]

Ocho [oh-cho]

Huit [weet]

Eight Ladybugs / **Ocho Mariquitas** / **Huit Coccinelles**
[ayt lay-dee-bugz]   [oh-cho ma-lee-kee-tas]   [weet kok-see-nell]

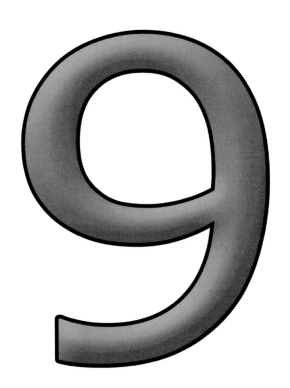

9 Nine [na-in]

Nueve [nuu-eh-veh]

Neuf [nuuf]

Nine Raccoons / Nueve Mapaches / Neuf Ratons Laveurs

[na-in rah-koonz]   [nuu-eh-veh ma-pah-chess]   [nuuf ra-taw la-vuur]

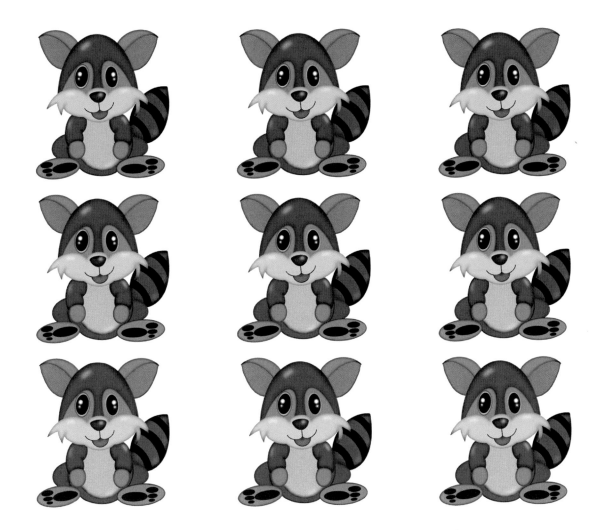

10

Ten [ten]

Diez [dee-ez]

Dix [dis]

Ten Eels / Diez Anguilas / Dix Anguilles
[ten eelz]   [dee-ez ang-gee-las]   [dis awng-gee]

11

Eleven [e-leh-ven]

Once [on-seh]

Onze [ouwz]

Eleven Newts / Once Tritónes / Onze Tritons

[e-leh-ven newts]   [on-seh tlee-toe-nes]   [ouwz tree-toe]

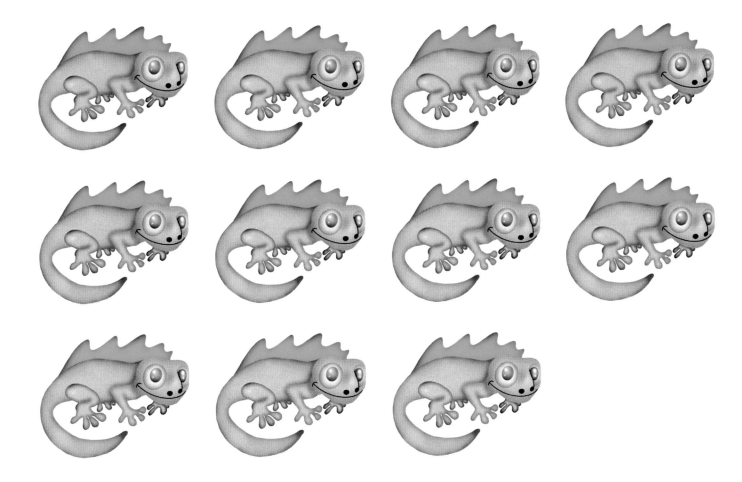

12

Twelve [tu-welv]
Doce [doh-seh]
Douze [dooz]

Twelve Giraffes / Doce Jirafas / Douze Girafes
[tu-welv ji-raafs]　　　[doh-seh he-raa-fas]　　　[dooz jee-haaf]

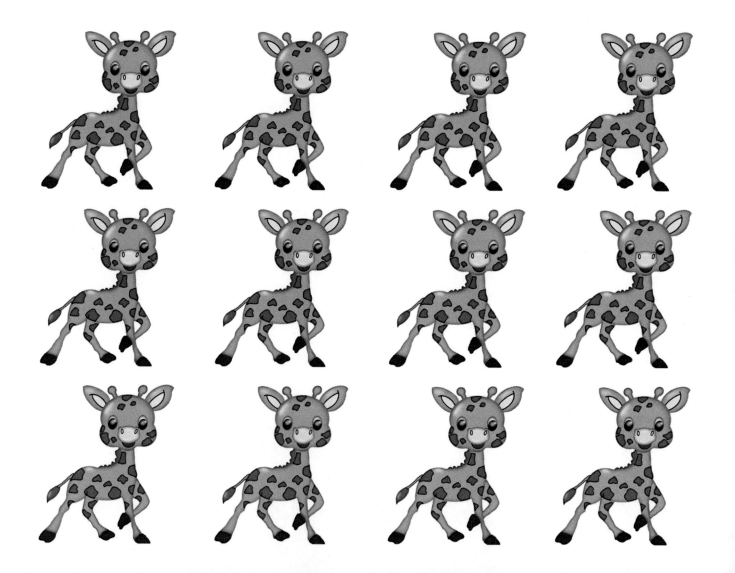

13

Thirteen [ther-teen]

Trece [tleh-seh]

Treize [trez]

Thirteen Mice / Trece Ratones / Treize Souris

[ther-teen mice]   [tleh-seh ra-toe-nes]   [trez su-ree]

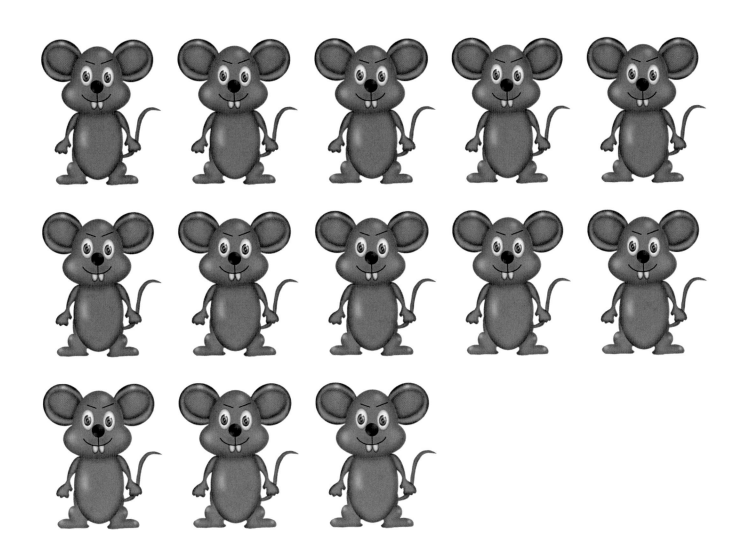

14

Fourteen [for-teen]

Catorce [ka-tol-seh]

Quatorze [ka-torz]

Fourteen Lions / Catorce Leones / Quatorze Lions
[for-teen ly-ons]   [ka-tol-seh ley-oh-nes]   [ka-torz lee-oh]

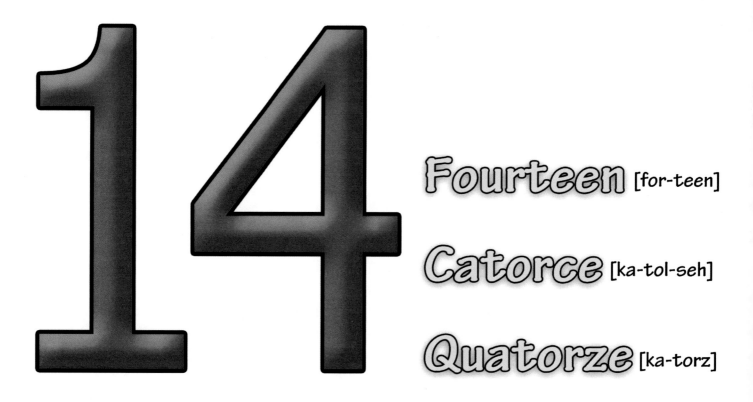

15

Fifteen [fif-teen]
Quince [kin-seh]
Quinze [kaanz]

Fifteen Butterflies / Quince Mariposas / Quinze Papillons
[fif-teen but-ter-flyz]　　[kin-seh ma-lee-po-sas]　　[kaanz pa-pee-yo]

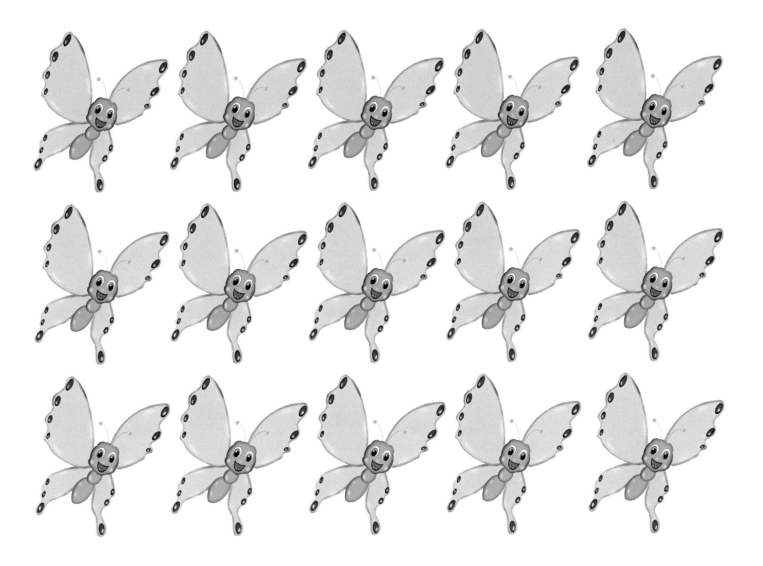

16

Sixteen [siks-teen]

Dieciséis [dee-eh-see-saes]

Seize [sayz]

Sixteen Monkeys / Dieciséis Monos / Seize Singes
[siks-teen mong-keez]   [dee-eh-see-saes mo-nos]   [sayz saaj]

17

Seventeen [seh-ven-teen]

Diecisiete [dee-eh-si-see-eh-teh]

Dix-sept [dis-set]

Seventeen Frogs / **Diecisiete Ranas** / **Dix-sept Crapauds**
[seh-ven-teen frogz]   [dee-eh-si-see-eh-teh raa-nas]   [dis-set kra-poe]

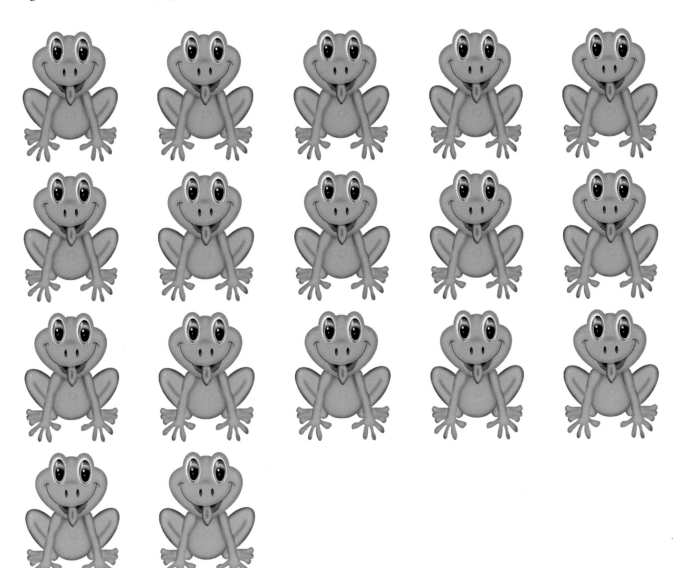

18

Eighteen [ae-teen]

Dieciocho [dee-eh-si-oh-cho]

Dix-huit [diz-wit]

Eighteen Ostriches / Dieciocho Avestruces / Dix-huit Autruches
[ae-teen os-tree-jiz]   [dee-eh-si-oh-cho ah-ves-tlu-ses]   [diz-wit ut-rish]

19

Nineteen [na-in-teen]

Diecinueve [dee-eh-si-nu-eh-veh]

Dix-neuf [diz-nuuf]

Nineteen Ducks / Diecinueve Patos / Dix-neuf Canards

[na-in-teen duks]   [dee-eh-si-nu-eh-veh pah-tos]   [diz-nuuf ka-naa]

20

Twenty [twen-tee]

Veinte [vae-in-teh]

Vingt [vah]

Twenty Zebras / Veinte Cebras / Vingt Zèbres

[twen-ti zee-braz]   [vae-in-teh say-blas]   [vah zae-bra]

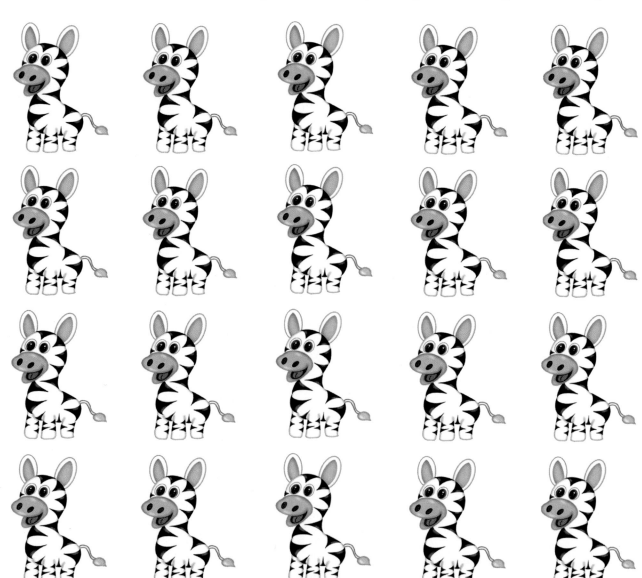

Let's PRACTICE
writing numbers

pratiquons l'écriture nombres

practiquemos escribir números

Use crayon to trace the numbers

Usa crayón para rastrear los números

Utiliser le crayon pour tracer les nombres

7	7
8	8
9	9

13	13
14	14
15	15

1919

2020

GREAT JOB LITTLE GENIUS!
YOU'RE AMAZING!

Let's
COLOR
vamos a colorear
nous allons colorer

Pig
[pig]

Cerdo
[sel-do]

Cochon
[ku-sho]

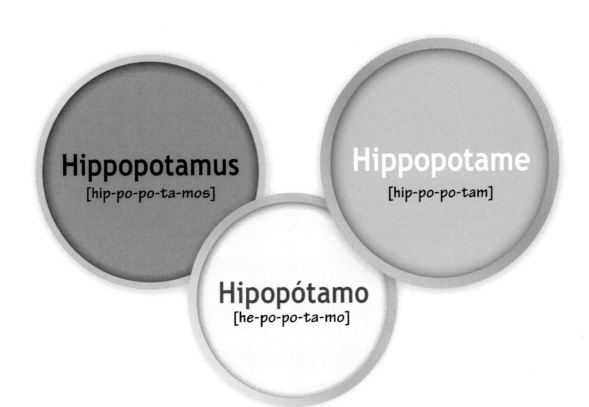

Hippopotamus
[hip-po-po-ta-mos]

Hippopotame
[hip-po-po-tam]

Hipopótamo
[he-po-po-ta-mo]

Koala
[ko-waa-la]

Coala
[ko-aah-la]

Koala
[ko-ah-la]

Gorilla
[goh-ril-la]

Gorila
[goh-ree-la]

Gorille
[gu-ree]

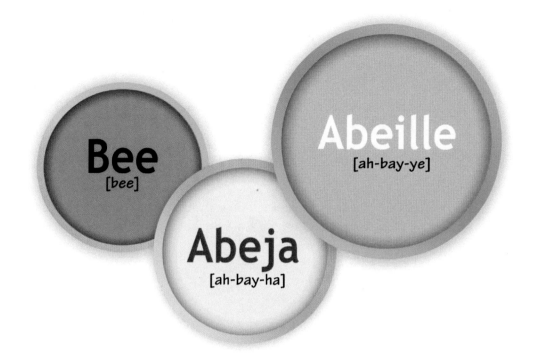

Bee
[bee]

Abeja
[ah-bay-ha]

Abeille
[ah-bay-ye]

Turtle
[ter-tle]

Tortuga
[tol-too-ga]

Tortue
[tok-tyu]

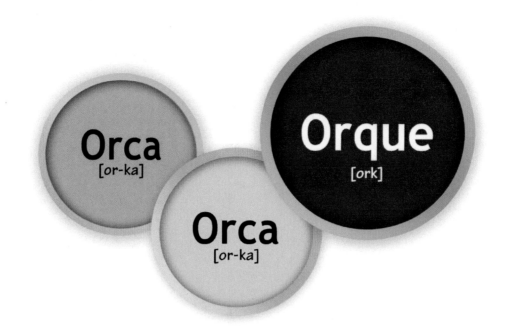

Orca
[or-ka]

Orca
[or-ka]

Orque
[ork]

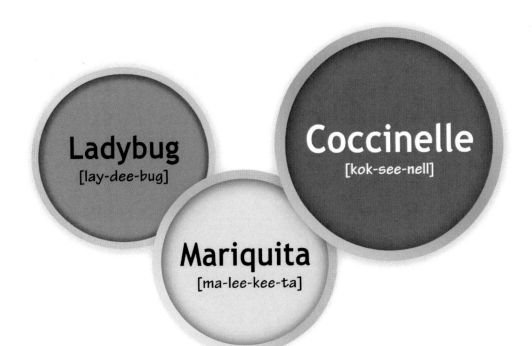

Ladybug
[lay-dee-bug]

Mariquita
[ma-lee-kee-ta]

Coccinelle
[kok-see-nell]

Raccoon
[rah-koon]

Mapache
[ma-paa-cheh]

Raton Laveur
[ra-taw la-vuur]

Eel
[eel]

Anguille
[ang-gee]

Anguila
[ang-gee-la]

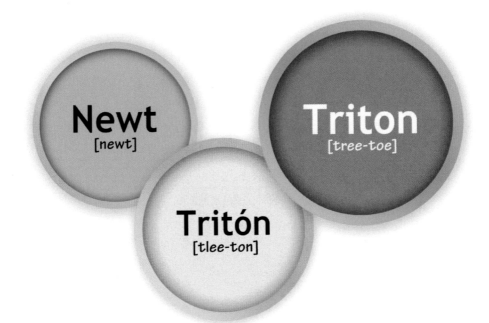

Newt
[newt]

Tritón
[tlee-ton]

Triton
[tree-toe]

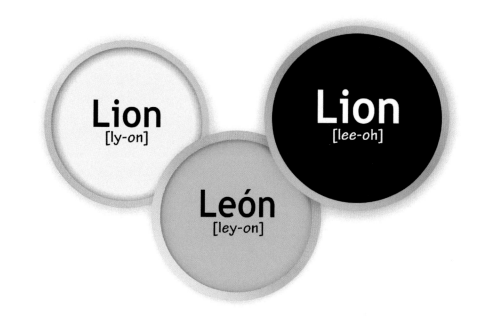

Lion
[ly-on]

Lion
[lee-oh]

León
[ley-on]

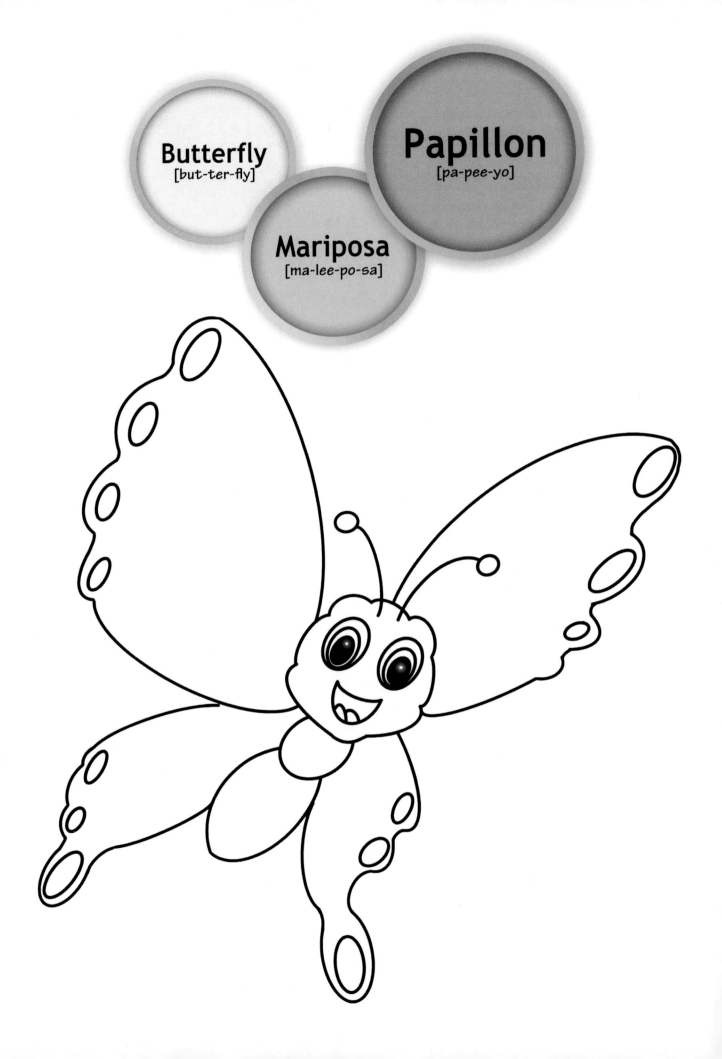

Butterfly
[but-ter-fly]

Mariposa
[ma-lee-po-sa]

Papillon
[pa-pee-yo]

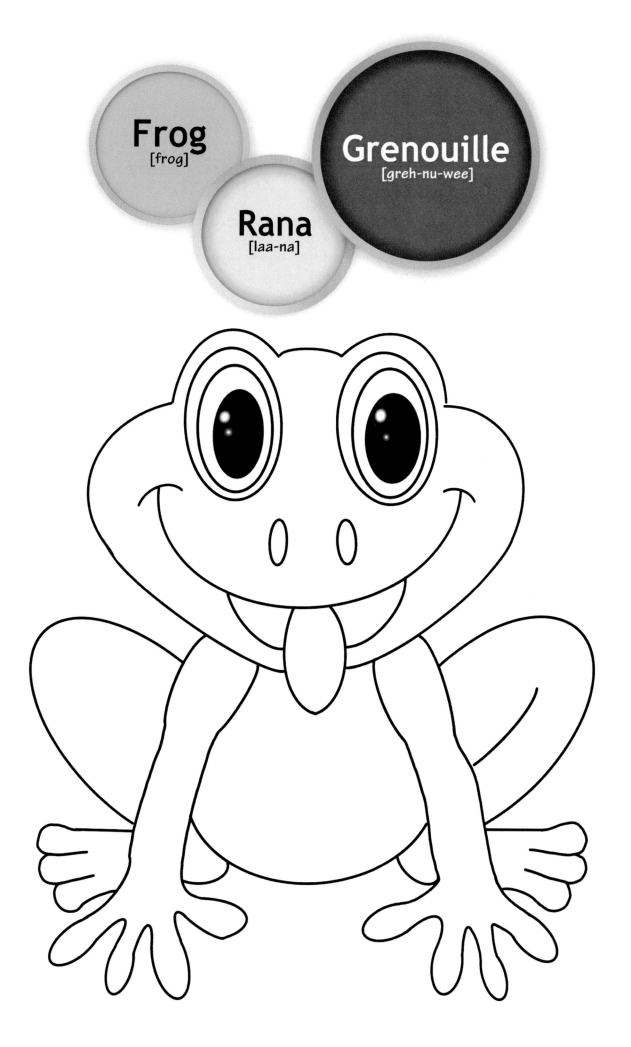

Walrus
[wal-rus]

Morsa
[mol-sa]

Morse
[mors]

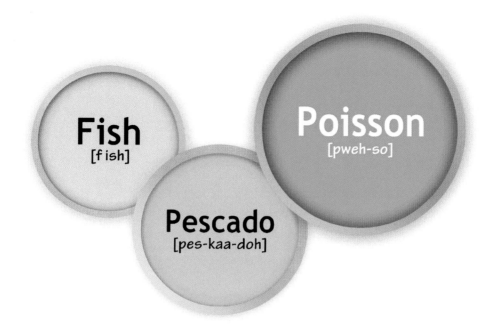

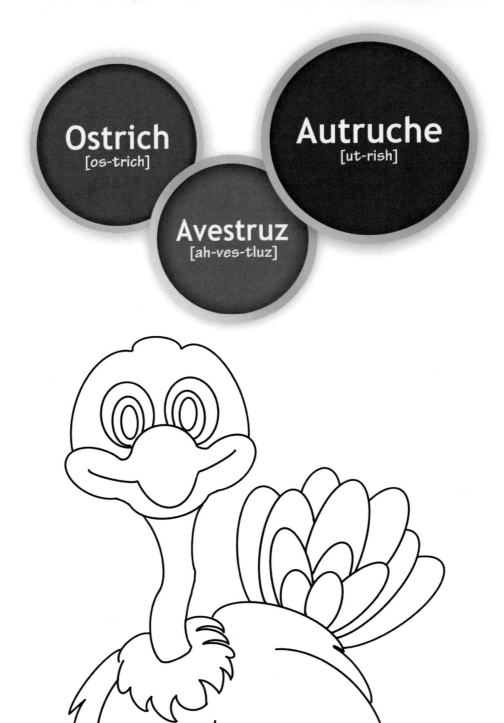

Ostrich
[os-trich]

Avestruz
[ah-ves-tluz]

Autruche
[ut-rish]

Vulture
[vol-cher]

Vautour
[vuu-tuo]

Buitre
[bwee-tleh]

Memory Bank

Banco de Memoria   Banque de Mémoire

Write the name of the animal on the dotted line.

Which animal is this?

Which animal is this?

Which animal is this?

Which
animal
is this?

Count the Animals

How many animals do you see in
each box? Can you count them?

Write the correct number on the line.

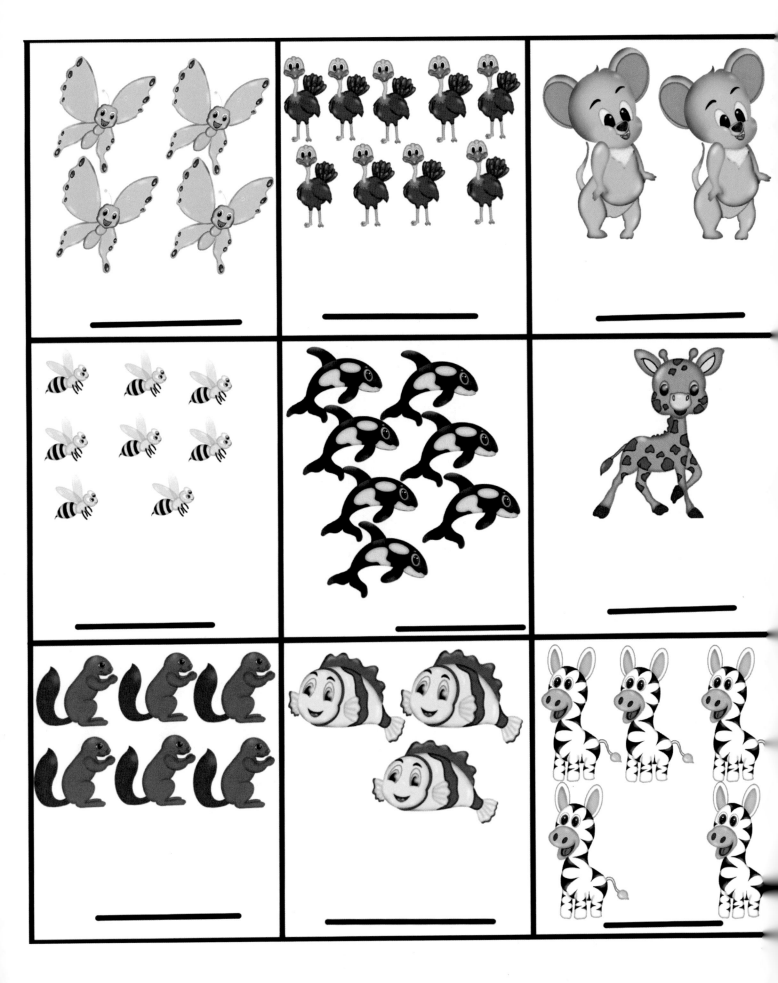

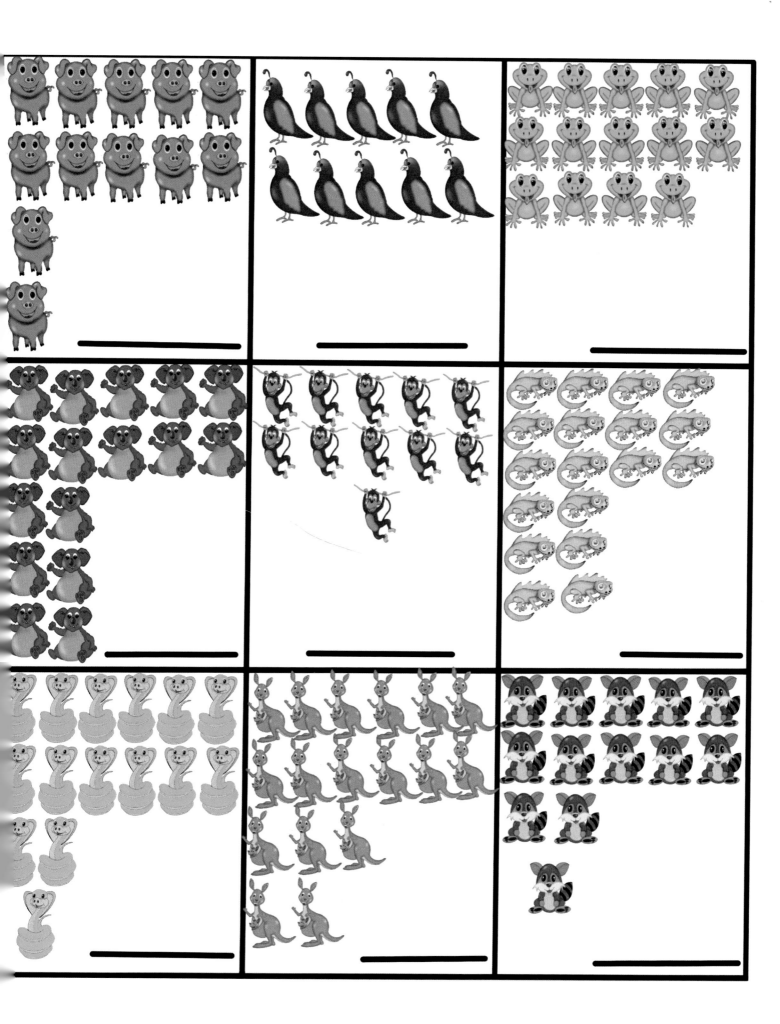

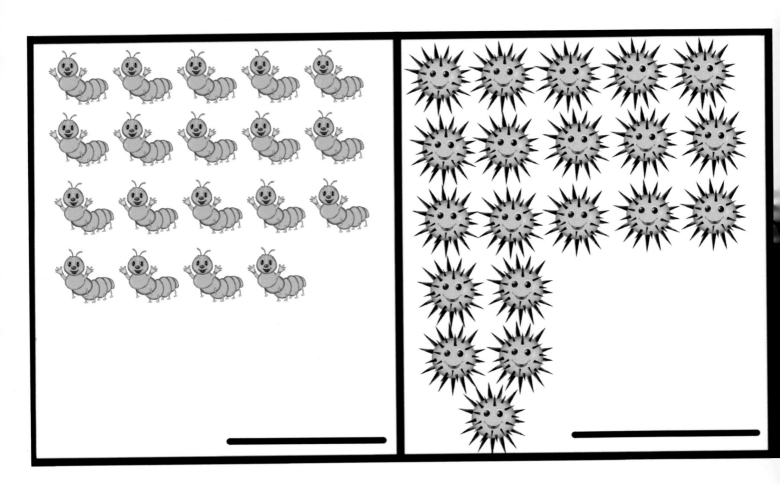

GAME INSTRUCTIONS

Cheese Quest is a two-player game. It is an early-stage education game which is designed to help children to develop their counting skills and engender a healthy competitive spirit in learning.

NB: A dice is needed to play. Each player needs a token.

1. To start the game, each player will select a start position at the top or bottom of the board where the mouse is standing.
2. Using the dice, each player will take turns to roll (any player can start). The player who rolls **SIX (6)** on the dice first, will start the game at number 1. The other player will start when the dice falls on SIX (6).
3. Players will move along the numbered path with their token based on the number they roll on the dice on their turn.
4. The player who reaches the cheese in the center first, wins the game!

The winner will say – "I got the cheese!"

Find the Number

Find the missing numbers and write them in the yellow box.

Use the numbers chart to help you find the correct number.

1
One | Uno | Un

2
Two | Dos | Deux

3
Three | Tres | Trois

4
Four | Cuatro | Quatre

5
Five | Cinco | Cinq

6
Six | Seis | Six

7
Seven | Siete | Sept

8
Eight | Ocho | Huit

9
Nine | Nueve | Neuf

10
Ten | Diez | Dix

11 Eleven | Once | Onze

12 Twelve | Doce | Douze

13 Thirteen | Trece | Treize

14 Fourteen | Catorce | Quatorze

15 Five | Quince | Quinze

16 Six | Dieciséis | Seize

17 Seven | Diecisiete | Dix-sept

18 Eight | Dieciocho | Dix-huit

19 Nine | Diecinueve | Dix-neuf

20 Ten | Veinte | Vingt

21
Twenty-one | Veintiuno | Vingt-et-un

22
Twenty-two | Veintidós | Vingt-deux

23
Twenty-three | Veintitrés | Vingt-trois

24
Twenty-four | Veinticuatro | Vingt- quatre

25
Twenty-five | Veinticinco | Vingt-cinq

26
Twenty-six | Veintiséis | Vingt-six

27
Twenty-seven | Veintisiete | Vingt-sept

28
Twenty-eight | Veintiocho | Vingt- huit

29
Twenty-nine | Veintinueve | Vingt-neuf

30
Thirty | Treinta | Trente

31
Thirty-one | Treinta y uno | Trente-et-un

32
Thirty-two | Treinta y dos | Trente-deux

33
Thirty-three | Treinta y tres | Trente-trois

34
Thirty-four | Treinta y cuatro | Trente-quatre

35
Thirty-five | Treinta y cinco | Trente-cinq

36
Thirty-six | Treinta y seis | Trente-six

37
Thirty-seven | Treinta y siete | Trente-sept

38
Thirty-eight | Treinta y ocho | Trente-huit

39
Thirty-nine | Treinta y nueve | Trente-neuf

40
Forty | Cuarenta | Quarante

41
Forty-one | Cuarenta y uno | Quarante-et-un

42
Forty-two | Cuarenta y dos | Quarante-deux

43
Forty-three | Cuarenta y tres | Quarante-trois

44
Forty-four | Cuarenta y cuatro | Quarante-quatre

45
Forty-five | Cuarenta y cinco | Quarante-cinq

46
Forty-six | Cuarenta y seis | Quarante-six

47
Forty-seven | Cuarenta y siete | Quarante-sept

48
Forty-eight | Cuarenta y ocho | Quarante-huit

49
Forty-nine | Cuarenta y nueve | Quarante-neuf

50
Fifty | Cincuenta | Cinquante

51

Fifty-one | Cincuenta y uno | Cinquante-et-un

52

Fifty-two | Cincuenta y dos | Cinquante-deux

53

Fifty-three | Cincuenta y tres | Cinquante-trois

54

Fifty-four | Cincuenta y cuatro | Cinquante-quatre

55

Fifty-five | Cincuenta y cinco | Cinquante-cinq

56

Fifty-six | Cincuenta y seis | Cinquante-six

57

Fifty-seven | Cincuenta y siete | Cinquante-sept

58

Fifty-eight | Cincuenta y ocho | Cinquante-huit

59

Fifty-nine | Cincuenta y nueve Cinquante-neuf

60

Sixty | Sesenta | Soixante

61
Sixty-one | Sesenta y uno | Soixante-et-un

62
Sixty-two | Sesenta y dos | Soixante-deux

63
Sixty-three | Sesenta y tres | Soixante-trois

64
Sixty-four | Sesenta y cuatro | Soixante-quatre

65
Sixty-five | Sesenta y cinco | Soixante-cinq

66
Sixty-six | Sesenta y seis | Soixante-six

67
Sixty-seven | Sesenta y siete | Soixante-sept

68
Sixty-eight | Sesenta y ocho | Soixante-huit

69
Sixty-nine | Sesenta y nueve | Soixante-neuf

70
Seventy | Setenta | Soixante-dix

71

Seventy-one | Setenta y uno | Soixante-et-onze

72

Seventy-two | Setenta y dos | Soixante-douze

73

Seventy-three | Setenta y tres | Soixante-treize

74

Seventy-four | Setenta y cuatro | Soixante-quatorze

75

Seventy-five | Setenta y cinco | Soixante-quinze

76

Seventy-six | Setenta y seis | Soixante-seize

77

Seventy-seven | Setenta y siete | Soixante-dix-sept

78

Seventy-eight | Setenta y ocho | Soixante-dix-huit

79

Seventy-nine | Setenta y nueve Soixante-dix-neuf

80

Eighty | Ochenta | Quatre-vingts

81

Eighty-one | Ochenta y uno | Quatre-vingt-un

82

Eighty-two | Ochenta y dos | Quatre-vingt-deux

83

Eighty-three | Ochenta y tres | Quatre-vingt-trois

84

Eighty-four | Ochenta y cuatro | Quatre-vingt-quatre

85

Eighty-five | Ochenta y cinco | Quatre-vingt-cinq

86

Eighty-six | Ochenta y seis | Quatre-vingt-six

87

Eighty-seven | Ochenta y siete | Quatre-vingt-sept

88

Eighty-eight | Ochenta y ocho | Quatre-vingt-huit

89

Eighty-nine | Ochenta y nueve | Quatre-vingt-neuf

90

Ninety | Noventa | Quatre-vingt-dix

91
Ninety-one | Noventa y uno | Quatre-vingt-onze

92
Ninety-two | Noventa y dos | Quatre-vingt-douze

93
Ninety-three | Noventa y tres | Quatre-vingt-treize

94
Ninety-four | Noventa y cuatro | Quatre-vingt-quatorze

95
Ninety-five | Noventa y cinco | Quatre-vingt-quinze

96
Ninety-six | Noventa y seis | Quatre-vingt-seize

97
Ninety -seven | Noventa y siete | Quatre-vingt-dix-sept

98
Ninety-eight | Noventa y ocho | Quatre-vingt-dix-huit

99
Ninety-nine | Noventa y nueve Quatre-vingt-dix-neuf

100
One Hundred | Cien | Cent

MORE BOOKS FOR KIDS BY JUST GENIOS KIDS
AVAILABLE ON AMAZON IN EBOOK AND PAPERBACK

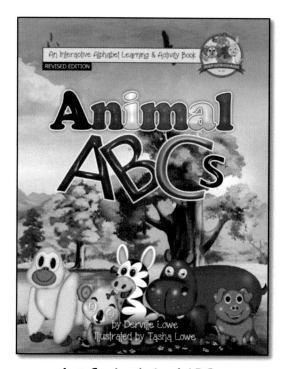

Just Genios Animal ABCs:
An Interactive Alphabet Learning &
Activity Book

Colour Me Beautiful
Colouring Book

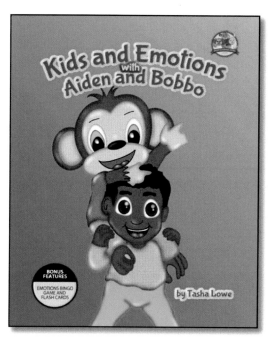

Kids and Emotions with Aiden and Bobbo
Fostering emotional intelligence in
children

Rex Gawn Ah Canada
Based on a true story of Jamaican dogs
who found a new home in Canada

I Have Autism but Autism Isn't Me
Uplifting persons with Autism and
raising awareness about ASD

Chloé Goes to the Zoo
An animal-loving girl with an
"I can" attitude

"Pretty for a Black Girl"
Affirming and uplifting black girls

SEND FEEDBACK, QUERIES, REQUESTS AND ORDERS TO
justgenios@gmail.com

FOLLOW JUST GENIOS ON INSTAGRAM
@just.genios

@JUSTGENIOSKIDS

Manufactured by Amazon.ca
Bolton, ON

36694554R00052